So Yummy

Cheap, Easy & Delicious

57 NO MEAT NO WORRY RECIPES

Beginners Wanted

Crystal Jones

KUDOS

*__Veronique Desormeaux__ of Cuisinique
for the first part of the book edits.
And __Crosslink Digitals__ for the
design & layout of this recipe book.*

CONTENTS

A POSITIVE NO-MEAT INTRODUCTION

Unlike a vegetarian diet, a plant-based wellness plan goes beyond meat-free, and replaces all animal food products with plant-based foods. Contrary to mainstream ideologies, the conscious rejection of meat and animal based products will not reduce your quality of life! It will bring about a wellness lifestyle that is all So Yummy.

The options that exist in the world of the alternative foods are so numerous that your plant-based diet plan has many delicious discoveries in store for you. It is not difficult to follow a healthy plant-based diet with a consistent meal plan – and you may say goodbye to excess pounds and hello, to newfound energy!.

A life without meat uses plant-based foods like fruits, vegetables, legumes, cereals, grains, potatoes, nuts, and seeds to provide you with the nutrients you need and enable you to eat a much more nutritious variety. Your no-meat diet plan lets you choose what and how you eat. With delicious and simple dishes, your new nutritional plan becomes your guide to better tastes and enjoyment of food. You will adapt to this new way of life and your cooking style will become simple, affordable and effortless, as you incorporate it into your daily activities.

This no-meat eating is currently very much in vogue, with many advantages. In practice, this means that you enjoy a lot of new variations and tasty alternatives but don't let this deter you. On the other hand, many people felt right at home, renewed, and revitalized after just a few days of switching to a meatless diet.

If you jump on board, understand you can eat as much as you want with plant-based foods like fruits, vegetables, grains, nuts and plant-based products.

If you enjoy the food substitution for a spaghetti dish without wheat or gluten-derived ingredients and substitute with (Konjac, Rice, quinoa, or chickpea flour) and if you desire "meat" balls, there are choices like soy, grain and vegetable versions, and nut versions. Above all, eating meatless requires creativity, which will be an enjoyable, healthy, and affordable journey. When you enjoy cooking, you can try out things and try something new every day.

Many foods that you presently enjoy such as spaghetti or other pasta products can be substituted with other delicious facsimiles such as rice, quinoa, chickpea flours, and a relatively new product called konjac.

There are also many substitutes for meatballs that use such ingredients like soy, grain, vegetable, and nut versions.

Being creative with these substitutions will lean you to new delicious tastes while maintaining healthier new choices.

The contents of this book will guide you through creative alternatives for your plant-based wellness journey whether you enjoy cooking or are simply starting out!

Instead of meat, you can buy meat-free products made with soy, grains, and nut variations. Above all, eating meatless requires creativity, which will be an enjoyable, healthy, and affordable journey. Enjoy this new level of eating, cooking and trying things out. Give your palette some new flavours, and try something new every day.

ABOUT THE AUTHOR

My name is Crystal Jones, and as a former body builder and competitor, I have come to realize how important good habits are and so I keep my exercise workouts up. I have made many transitions in my life including my food choices. I have tried many ways to eat. I have tried the fruitarian diet, a high protein diet like Atkins, Macrobiotic diets and food combining

Writing books on the topic of Raw food, Avocados, Smoothies, and Organic Natural Skin Care have refined my choices for the better. Applying these improvements in my life has helped me eliminate joint pain, gas and bloating and I have even lost weight during the pandemic.

I have more vitality, energy and stamina. I love eating NO MEAT meals and I am sticking with it as it works. I have so much fun in the kitchen testing recipes and then putting them into words for you.

I think this book So Yummy is a winner and I hope you do too.

Make better food choices which leads to better nutrition.

Listen to my podcast - **https://tinyurl.com/4pzbex64**

You can visit my personal website here: **http://crystaljoneslive.com**

Be Well,

Crystal Jones

CHAPTER ONE
Going Meatless
For Beginners

Here is a Quick Startup Guide for Meatless Beginners

1. Before you start eliminating from your diet, START by increasing your intake of tofu, whole grains, beans, legumes, nuts, and seeds.

2. Learn the proper techniques for preparation, storage, and use.
3. Start preparing and planning a meal for some of the quick and easy vegan dishes you might like from this book.
4. Begin by replacing dairy beverages with non-dairy options.
5. Select alternative beverages like organic soy beverages. Almond, cashew, and oat products that is unflavored and unsweetened.

> *People mistakenly believe that having NO MEAT is not about saying "NO" but it's about saying "YES" to better-eating choices in food and living."*

Nearly everyone in practically any age group can successfully meet their nutritional needs with a balanced, well-planned vegan diet.

ONE STEP AT A TIME:
- Increase your intake of tofu, whole grains, beans, legumes, nuts, and seeds.
- Cut out meat products, gradually including fish and poultry, from your diet.
- Many choose to cut out dairy, cheese, eggs, and honey when they feel ready. Work at one food group at a time at your own pace.

Examine plant-based options:

Many individuals discover that switching entirely to plant-based proteins like vegan burgers, vegan hot dogs, vegan cheeses, etc., can make the transition easier.

Benefits of Eating NO MEAT

People choose to become vegans in different stages in their life in their youth or as an adult. So many incredible ways that eating a NO MEAT may improve our lives, including astonishing health advantages, reduced environmental impact, better resource management, and many more.

It is understandable why many individuals are adopting a NO MEAT diet. There are a number of people who have become captivated with the idea of living a cleaner, and greener lifestyle.

A great benefit of a NO MEAT diet is that it significantly reduces the fat in your diet. Consuming excessive amounts of dairy and meats is closely associated with fat; by eliminating significant amounts of fat from your diet, you can significantly enhance your physical health and your ability to lose weight. If you have been finding it challenging to manage your weight effectively, this can give you plenty of reasons to reduce your meat intake.

Wise Suggestions & Reminders

Don't let yourself get too stressed out making the transition. Take your time, can't get stressed. Be ready to learn from your mistakes and keep going, don't get stressed; be patient with yourself. Adopting a meatless lifestyle is not that challenging, and keep moving in the right direction; just the fact you are reducing your animal/meat consumption is terrific.

You will be aware that there are so many incredible plant-based food choices available at present you might be surprised by the variety.

- **Fresh & Frozen Produce:**
Fresh fruit is best when purchased locally and eaten at its prime. But during the off-season purchasing frozen fruit or freezing your fruit and vegetables is an excellent choice. You can enjoy frozen fruits in breakfast oatmeal, baking and smoothies.

Keeping the nutrients within while it is transported to your local grocer. This also means the produce keeps a longer shelf life and is less likely to go to waste.

- **Organic & Non-Organic:**
You are free to choose whether to purchase organic products. Organic foods are typically more expensive. Check out the organic

area even if you don't often buy organic produce, as it often goes on sale, add a tip about how to wash non-organic fruits and vegetables.

TIP: _Cleaning Fruits & Vegetables_
1. Wash under cold water using a soft cloth or brush is very effective.
2. Soak in saltwater solution for 20 minutes to remove common pesticides and then rinse.
3. Another option is to soak for fruit or vegetables in a sink for 10 minutes. Using a vinegar soak (4 parts water to 1 part vinegar). Then rinse thoroughly.

- **Vegetables:**

Invest in a few raw vegetables to add to salads, wraps, sandwiches, or dips. Purchase a minimum of two leafy greens for salads, wraps, and sandwiches or steam, roast, sauté, or stir fry.

Frozen vegetables are also a good choice as they save on spoilage and are a fantastic healthy backup alternative if you don't have time to shop.

- **Fruits:**

Fruit from frozen can be used in baking and smoothies (pre-frozen fruit for topping oatmeal or non-dairy yogurts). Dried fruit can be used in baking, as a garnish for breakfast cereal, and as a portable snack when combined with nuts or trail mix.

- **Grains, Beans, & Legumes:**

Keep at least two bakery items on hand and keep them handy in your refrigerator and defrost single portions as needed. These goods freeze well.

Keep a few kinds of legumes, beans, and fermented foods in addition to two or three whole grains or starches. For a full meal, mix and match them and serve with a vegetable side dish.

Having oatmeal on hand makes it easy to prepare nutritious meals, smoothies, and baked goods. Try going for the least processed option, like the old fashion rolled oats or the steel-cut varieties and avoid the instant.

So Yummy – Let's Get Started

Starch Suggestions
- Bread choices include (just a few: gluten free, wheat, teff, sorghum, millet, or flax)
- Taco shells - corn or cauliflower
- Pancake mix – gluten free or other
- Pitas
- Noodles – durum semolina, chickpea, lentil and konjac

Whole Grains & Starches
- Barley
- Rice – wild rice, brown rice, basmati, jasmine, black rice
- Buckwheat
- Bulgur (cracked wheat)
- Millet
- Oatmeal
- Corn
- Rye
- Teff

- Quinoa
- Sorghum
- Farro

Beans & Legumes
- Garbanzo beans, often known as chickpeas (canned/dry)
- Peanuts
- Navy beans (canned/dry)
- Peas, green
- Edamame (frozen)
- Kidney beans
- Pinto bean
- Lima beans
- Soybeans
- Lentils

Soy Products
- Tempeh
- Miso
- Natto
- Organic Soymilk
- Marinated or smoked tofu
- Tofu - Firm – Soft
- Soy sauce and white soy sauce (shoyu sauce)
- Amino Acids – coconut or soy

Healthy Fats & Oils

Healthy fats are an essential component of a vegan diet! To ensure a healthy balance of omega 3 and 6 essential fatty acids, incorporate various items from this list.

Some whole foods, such as avocado, dark chocolate, nuts, seeds, or olives, should always be available for snacking. You should also always have a few different oils on hand for cooking and making salad dressings. Keep on hand at least one nut or seed butter for dipping fruit or adding to oatmeal or just as a spread on toast.

Some Suggestions To Stock Up On:
- Chia seeds
- Avocados
- Dark chocolate
- Coconut milk
- Hummus
- Nuts
- Olives

Oils
- Hemp seed oil
- Avocado oil
- Olive oil
- Coconut oil
- Grapeseed oil
- Flax seed oil
- Peanut oil
- Sesame oil
- Canola oil
- Sunflower oil
- Vegan "butter"

Raw Nuts & Seeds
- Almonds
- Pumpkin seeds
- Poppy seeds
- Cashews
- Brazil nuts
- Flax seeds
- Cashew nuts
- Hazelnuts
- Sunflower seeds

- Macadamias
- Sesame seeds
- Pecans
- Pine nuts
- Chia seeds
- Tahini (sesame butter)
- Pistachios
- Walnuts

"So Yummy" Condiments

It's simple to vary your meals when you have a variety of condiments, herbs, and spices available.

Buy smaller quantities of dried spices or herbs from the bulk department if you don't use them frequently. Wash any leftover fresh herbs you won't use immediately and freeze them.

Sweeteners
- Stevia
- Dates
- Dried fruits
- Molasses
- Fruit preserves
- Coconut sugar
- Organic cane sugar
- Maple syrup
- Dark chocolate chips
- Agave syrup

Herbs & Spices
- Black peppercorns and grinder
- Cumin
- Smoked Paprika
- Turmeric
- Basil

- Rosemary
- Garlic
- Oregano
- Cumin
- Chili powder
- Thyme
- Cayenne
- Salt – sea salt, Himalayan salt (pink salt), celtic salt

Condiments
- Lemon or lime juice
- Mustard
- Salsa
- White Vinegar
- Apple Cider Vinegar
- Balsamic Vinegar
- Nutritional yeast
- Hummus
- Sriracha or chili sauce
- Vegan mayo
- Soy sauce
- Vegetable bouillon cubes, or powder

Cooking & Baking
- Organic coconut oil
- Vegan Butter
- Yeast
- Baking soda
- Apple cider vinegar
- Coconut flour
- Whole grain flour
- Ground flax seed
- Spelt flour
- Almond flour
- Baking powder

CHAPTER TWO
Useful Kitchen Essentials

For Beginners, Home Cooks And Kitchen Chefs

Many kitchen gadgets are available to make life easier; whether you switch from a meatless to a plant-based diet, there is always room for improvement in cooking.

Many home cook kitchens should have this, and you may find it a useful starting point.

- **High-Speed Blender &/or Food Processor**
Although a food processor and a blender may appear interchangeable, each appliance has its own role. It pays to consider the types of food you're most likely to prepare and prioritize which gadget you will use the most.

A high-speed blender is your best option if the items you prepare have a more liquid consistency, including soups, smoothies, or frozen desserts.

On the other hand, food processors are best used for chopping foods like vegetables, nuts, legumes, combining dry items or creating a non-meat meatball. Most blenders and food processors may be used to whip up a cream base, like vegan mayonnaise, or blend dips like hummus. However, these appliances are typically not necessary if you have space in your kitchen for both of these, they are some of the top tools used in kitchens and will be beneficial to your wellness food journey.

- **Handheld Mixer**

A handheld mixer is a portable electric appliance with two detachable metal beaters and adjustable speeds. Even if you don't cook or bake a lot, it is necessary and useful for any kitchen. It is used to whip, beat, mix, and blend a range of dishes. Because of its portability and convenience, you may put it in your cupboard while not in use, thanks to its small size.

- **Stainless Steel Knife Set**

Nothing can help you prepare fresh vegetables easily and more rapidly than using a good set of cutlery. You will want quality stainless steel blades to slice, dice and mince your vegetables and chop your fresh herbs.

You will want handles and blades of superior quality and precision control; be sure to test and feel if it is right for you.

Purchase a stainless-steel knife set or buy them separately and be sure it includes a paring knife, bread knife, chef knife (made in Germany or France and heavier to hold – some feature a grant on edge) or santoku (made in Japan – balanced weight and lighter to hold), utility knife, and a sharpening steel to keep your knives sharp and in tip-top shape.

Every kitchen uses 3-5 knives the most frequently. Additionally, people pick quality knives for their fine detailing and superior performance when cooking meals. They also make a great present for aspiring or seasoned chefs.

- **A Must-Have Kitchen Scissors**

Kitchen scissors are a practical tool to chop up your herbs and seasonings to the perfect size before cooking, mixing, or juicing. Cutting off the ends and removing green or inedible sections you don't want in your food. Kitchen scissors are great as they make things quick and simple.

- **Measuring Cups & Spoons**

For baking or cooking, measuring cups and spoons guarantee accurate and consistent measurement for all recipes, ensuring the right quantities and assisting in providing great outcomes.

Each measuring cup or spoon's volume is marked to ensure the right one is used for baking or cooking.
- Measuring spoons (¼ t, ½t, 1t, 1T)
- Dry measuring cups (¼, ⅓, ½, 1 cup)
- Liquid measuring cups (I have 2 cups & 4 cups)

- **Whisk**

A hand whisk is essential for combining liquids like oil and vinegar.

- **Ladle**

This large spoon tool helps stir liquids and foods in large pots. It is a necessary all-purpose tool for soups and stews when scooping, mixing, and holding meals in place while working on it.

- **Cutting Boards**

A kitchen tool with a hard surface typically constructed of wood, wood laminate, composite materials or plastic used as a surface for slicing, dicing, dicing, or mincing food goods.

- **Mixing Bowls And Colanders**

Mixing bowls are useful in the kitchen as they come in various sizes and are easier to handle and prepare meals. Given its strength and longevity with heavy usage and regular washing in the kitchen, stainless steel is the favoured choice.

Add the colander to your kitchen to rinse and drain your food quickly and easily.

- **Vegetable Peeler - Zester & Grater**

A peeler does exactly what its name suggests: peels the skin of fruits and vegetables. Peelers often feature a steel blade linked to a steel, metal, rubber, or plastic handle.

A zester is only used for citrus fruits to flavour up recipes. On the other hand, a grater is always used to shred vegetables.

- **Skillets - Pots And Pans**

A shallow skillet is sometimes known as a frying pan or a frying pan. Using a skillet is a common way to stir-fry or sauté food, a culinary technique that involves cooking food quickly in a small amount of oil and frequently at high heat.

Their sizes and shapes are one way the two are different. Pots have higher sidewalls and are deeper. Their sides often rise straight up, and their base is round. In contrast, a pan is quite shallow.

- **Spatula**

A spatula is an appliance for the kitchen that can be used to mix, scrape, flip, or spread items.

- **Rolling Pin**

Rolling pins are a necessary appliance in the kitchen, used to flatten a variety of dough evenly, including those for pies, pastries, cookies, and pasta.

- **Tongs**

This tool is available in small or big sizes, with metal ends. Tongs are useful for picking up food of any shape or size, especially when food is hot. With the help of tongs, the cook may move it about, place it from the pot or pan and then serve without risking hand burns.

- **Bakeware Items**

Bakeware is a phrase used to describe various baking tools, including baking dishes, baking pans, and baking sheets. They all have in common that they are all used to baking different sweet or savory dishes in the oven. Most bakeware is metal, glass or ceramic, but silicone is now utilized to make some of these baked goods; various types, sizes, and shapes of bakeware are available. Cookie sheets, cake pans, jelly-roll pans, tube pans, loaf pans, muffin tins, Bundt pans, brioche molds, spring form pans, tart pans, pie plates, square and rectangular bakers, round and oval casseroles, ramekins, and pizza pans are a few examples of things that fall under the category of bakeware. Various things can be categorized as bakeware, many of which are used in extremely specific circumstances.

- **Spiralizer**

The raw fruits and vegetables are sliced into various spirals type noodles or zoodles shapes using the spiralizer's thin blades. Used for vegetables zucchini, sweet potatoes, beets, carrots, potatoes, turnips, broccoli ends, butternut squash, summer squash, onions, and even.

- **Nut Milk Bag or Cheesecloth**

With the assistance of the nut milk bag, you can easily create fresh, healthy beverages from nuts like almond and cashew milk.

- **Dehydrator**

A food dehydrator removes moisture from fresh fruit, vegetables, and herbs to preserve them. Fruits and vegetables suitable for drying include apples, pears, peaches, plums, apricots, strawberries, blueberries, carrots, celery, corn, green beans, potatoes, and tomatoes. Fruits can be dried and made into fruit leathers and rolls.

- **Air Fryer**

A common kitchen tool for air frying meals, including without using too much oil. Many use it for French fries or chips. It is like a convection oven; it can create a crunchy, crispy exterior, and it is a healthy alternative to deep frying.

- **Slow Cooker Or Crockpot**

While most conventional slow cooker pots are made of thick ceramic and heat from the bottom and the sides, the foods that can be cooked are vegan chili con carne, vegetable, cabbage, bean, onion, mushroom soup or minestrone. Vegetable curry stews, and so much more.

- **Salad Spinner & Colandler**

A salad spinner is a kitchen appliance used to drain extra liquid or water from leafy vegetables like lettuce, kale or other greens. Salad spinners it is comparable to a colander and is where you put the fresh greens and spin them.

- **Strainer**

An essential piece of cooking equipment mostly used to separate liquids from solids but may also be used to sift fine ingredients from coarse ones. The strainer can be made from many materials, like metal, nylon, or cotton, and can take the form of a spoon-shaped tool or a basket-shaped strainer; the choice is yours.

CHAPTER THREE
Cooking Skills For "So Yummy" Recipes

I mprove your cooking skills and switch from being a novice home cook to a master chef: no magic, no shortcuts, and no tricks. Minor adjustments can have a significant impact. We've compiled the most straightforward tips to boost your kitchen game.

- **Read Your Recipe Thoroughly**

Before gathering ingredients and utensils, carefully read the recipe's ingredients, instructions, and any notes. If you don't strictly adhere to the instructions, the food won't turn out correctly. Don't skim any part of the recipe; thoroughly read it and reread it. Visualize the process and remember the pictures. Even a pro can mess up if he doesn't bother to read the recipe. Keep the recipe handy, while cooking, not to overlook a step or the amount of an ingredient that must be added.

- **Get Well Organized**

Every cooking operation, from baking to plating, may be made faster by keeping a tidy environment. A clean, well-organized workspace is a good starting point for excellence in the kitchen. Nothing works better than the organization to boost productivity, cut waste, and adhere to food safety and hygiene standards! This level of organization will make even the most novices feel and appear like competent professionals.

- **Use "Mise En Place" (Means Putting Things In Place)**

Before you begin cooking, your ingredients should be washed, prepared/cut and measured. This is known as the French term "mise en place". All ingredients, tools, pans and bowls are laid out. This allows you to focus on your cooking and enjoy the process that much more. Chefs utilize this method to prepare a high volume of meals, efficiently.

- **Clean As You Cook**

Remember to properly clean and maintain cookware if you want to master the kitchen and keep your workspace pristine. Cleaning counters, wiping off your cutting board, and removing unnecessary stuff will significantly impact you! After creating a delicious meal, dealing with a mess may be a tremendous challenge.

- **Taste As You Go**

As you cook, flavors grow and alter. As moisture evaporation occurs, something may get saltier, or as a dish cook longer, the acid content may decrease. It's crucial to taste as you go to determine whether extra salt, acid, or any other spice is necessary. Because flavor develops gradually, don't wait until a dish is virtually done. Taste again and again as you go through the process, so the end result will be So Yummy!

- **Have Patience**

Being patient is a virtue, particularly while cooking. It will make all the difference in how your cuisine turns out to take your time to do things correctly, whether that means gently incorporating ingredients into a recipe rather than adding them all at once or patiently waiting for the dough to rise.

It's okay if a recipe doesn't turn out perfectly the first time. Making a dish that wasn't flawless taught you some lessons, and you can use what you discovered to handle it more expertly the next time you try it. Additionally, you'll feel good about yourself for sticking with it! Fortunately, scheduling your dishes to be ready all at once will be a breeze once you have had plenty of practice.

- **Be Attentive**

Concentrating prevents food from burning and becoming overly rigid or dry, and you can avoid getting hurt by cuts or burns. What scent does the food that you're cooking have? How does it appear? Seconds can sometimes determine whether a meal is a success or a flop. Moreover, the kitchen, which is also the center of your house, can be shockingly deadly. Consider that a kitchen has sharp blades, heated, exposed surfaces, boiling pots, and pans of sizzling grease. So be careful, stay attentive to everything around you, and strictly follow safety tips to prevent you from becoming a statistic for kitchen injuries.

- **Use Fresh Ingredients**

Compared to processed meals, your food might keep much more nutrients when cooking with fresh ingredients. Always try to avoid processed foods and, whenever possible, utilize fresh ingredients to boost your health. Fresh herbs and toasted spices are equally as essential to a tasty cuisine as fresh fruits and vegetables: Using vibrant, aromatic properties, they can make meals stand out. We eat with our eyes; science proves our eyes are the first point in the experience of food and drink. Unappetizing-looking food will not be eaten.

- **Watch Others**

You can learn to cook more quickly by paying attention to individuals you hold in high regard as the best chefs. You will know more and develop a broader range of cooking skills as you observe the cooks you respect and learn how and what they prepare. This relationship is significant because it may also result in happier cooking! Cook with a companion, be someone's chef and observe their manner, pick up how they talk about flavors and learn their secrets and suggestions!

This includes anyone who bakes, makes appetizers, and prepares meatless meals for the family. That's a lot of fun.

- **Practice Plating**

Although appearances aren't everything, they matter in the kitchen. Learning how to plate your food properly can make your culinary masterpieces stand out and give you a fun technique to impress your dinner guests.

CHAPTER FOUR
So Yummy
Recipes

Enjoy...

Homemade Vanilla Granola

Servings: 8
Total time: 40 mins

Ingredients
- 2 cups rolled oats (certified gluten-free)
- 2 cups chopped nuts (walnuts, almonds or pecans)
- 1 tsp cinnamon
- ¼ cup coconut oil
- ⅓ cup honey (or maple syrup, if vegan)
- 1 tbsp vanilla

Options: add dried fruit like cranberries, raisins, chia seeds, flax, and coconut flakes.

Preparation
- To begin, preheat your oven to 300 and line a baking pan with parchment paper.

- In a large mixing bowl, add your dry ingredients (oats, nuts, cinnamon) and stir them together.
- In a small, microwave-safe bowl, add your coconut oil and microwave till melted (about 1 minute). Add your honey, whisk them together, and microwave them again till they are very warm (about another 30-60 seconds). Add your vanilla and whisk it.
- Pour your wet ingredients over your dry ingredients and stir till all of your oats and nuts are covered entirely. Pour your granola onto your pan and spread it out into one thin, even layer. Bake in the oven for 25-30 minutes or till the edges are just starting to gain a bit of color. The granola will get crunchy as it cools.
- Let the granola cool entirely before breaking it up into pieces. Devour!

Delicious Pancakes
Sugar Free & Gluten Free

Servings: 10
Total time: 20 mins

Ingredients
- 1 cup oat flakes
- 2 teaspoons baking powder
- 1 tsp cinnamon
- 2 teaspoons ground vanilla
- ¼ tsp salt
- 2 bananas
- 1 cup plant beverage (oat, almond, cashew or organic soy)
- 2 tbsp date paste
- 1 tbsp coconut oil

Preparation
- Process the oat flakes into flour in a blender
- Mix the dry ingredients together.

- In a separate bowl, mash the bananas and mix in the remaining liquid ingredients.
- Mix everything together to form a doughy consistency.
- Pan-fry the pancakes in a pan over medium heat for about 1-2 minutes per side.
- Enjoy plain, or garnish with date paste, choice of fruit berries, strawberries, and bananas. Drizzle pure maple syrup.

"Egg Like" Scrambler

Servings: 2
Total time: 15 mins

Ingredients
- 1 package tofu natural, firm
- ½ onion
- ½ tsp himalayan salt
- ½ tsp turmeric powder (important for the yellow color)
- ¼ tsp pepper (to taste)
- ¼ tsp paprika powder (optional to taste)
- ¼ tsp garlic powder (optional to taste)
- 1 tbsp yeast flakes (optional to taste)
- ¼ cup of oat milk unsweetened, or alternatively plain yogurt
- 1 tbsp of chives (finely chopped)

Preparation
- Press the tofu block to dry between a clean kitchen towel and then crumble it into a bowl with your hands. Alternatively, mash with a fork (or potato masher).

- Peel and finely chop the onion and sauté in a well-coated, heated pan for 2-3 minutes until translucent.
- Add the tofu crumbs and fry for about 3-5 minutes.
- Add spices, fry for about 5 more minutes, stirring occasionally, and finally, stir in the unsweetened plant-based milk. Turn the heat down and let it steep for a few minutes until the liquid is absorbed.
- Finally, season with spices, sprinkle with chopped chives and enjoy immediately or store in an airtight container in the refrigerator for up to 3 days.

Strawberry Banana
Smoothie Bowl

Servings: 1
Total time: 10 mins

Ingredients
- 1 banana (frozen)
- 1 cup of strawberries (fresh or frozen)
- 1 cup of coconut, oat, or almond milk
- ¼ oat flakes (gluten-free possible)
- approximate ½ cup of nuts (and other toppings of your choice, (crunchy granola or muesli)

Preparation
- In the blender, add the liquid first, then the frozen fruit, and blend
- until the desired consistency is achieved.
- Put the rolled oats and/or granola in a bowl, fill up with the smoothie and sprinkle with toppings of your choice and enjoy.

Hazelnut "No-Tella" Spread - Sugar-free

Servings: 4
Total time: 10 mins

Ingredients
- 2 cups organic dates (pitted and soaked)
- ½ cup of water
- 1 cup of hazelnuts raw or roasted
- 4 tbsp cocoa powder (more if needed)
- ½ tsp ground vanilla or vanilla extract

Preparation

- Add to the blender water (here, you can use the soaking water from the dates). Add the hazelnuts in a blender at the highest setting to make hazelnut milk.
- Then add the drained dates and the remaining ingredients and mix again at the highest level until you get an even, creamy consistency.
- Depending on the power of the mixer, add extra water until the mixture turns by itself.
- Spread on toast, pancakes, or crackers. (See recipe for making Nutty Butters)
- Pour the mixture into a reusable glass container, seal and store it in the fridge. Use within 1 week.

Garlic Ginger Broccoli & Mushrooms Tofu Delish

Servings: 4 - 6
Total time: 20 mins

Ingredients
- 1-2 blocks of firm tofu (press out water & drained)
- 3 tsp of cornstarch
- 4-5 cremini mushrooms (sliced)
- 3 cups of broccoli florets (chopped)
- 1 red bell pepper (sliced)
- 1 yellow bell pepper (sliced)
- 2 tbsp of grapeseed oil
- 1 tsp of garlic powder
- ½ cup of raw cashews
- ½ tsp of salt and fresh ground pepper
- 2 tbsp of dark sesame oil – for cooking

Sauce for Stir Fry
- 2 tsp of soy sauce (low sodium)

- 3 tsp of hoisin sauce
- 2 tbsp of maple syrup
- 2 tbsp of rice wine vinegar
- 5 cloves of garlic (minced)
- 2-inch knob of grated ginger
- ½ cup of filtered water

Preparation
- Cube the tofu and add 1 tsp of cornstarch, garlic powder, thyme & salt and pepper and place in a glass container – shake until tofu is well coated.
- In a medium size mixing bowl, whisk together the stir fry until it is all well combined.
- Heat a large skillet on medium heat with the sesame oil, and add the tofu mixture to cook until golden brown on all sides.
- Once the tofu is cooked, add the mushrooms and stir frequently. Once the mushrooms are cooked, add the broccoli and sliced red peppers and cook until slightly firm.
- Next, pour the stir fry sauce for about 1-2 minutes until all ingredients are well coated
- Add cashews last into the saucepan.
- Remove from heat, serve & enjoy.

"So Yummy" Tabouli Salad With Cucumber & Chickpeas

Servings: 4
Total time: 20 mins

Ingredients

- 3 cups of flat-leaf parsley (finely chopped)
- 2 cloves garlic (minced)
- juice of 2 fresh lemons
- 1 cup cooked quinoa (1 ¾ cup of water for every cup of quinoa)
- ¼ cup of mint leaves (finely chopped)
- 8-10 cherry tomatoes (cut in half)
- 5 green onions (finely chopped)
- ½ cup of chickpeas (drained & rinsed)
- ¼ of extra virgin oil
- ½ cup of cucumber (diced)
- pinch of sea salt

Preparation

- In a medium size, pot brings to boil 1 ¾ cup of water to every cup of quinoa. (If there is too much water, it will go mushy. If too little, it will be too dry). Simmer for 15 minutes. Remove the pot from the heat and let it sit covered for 10 minutes more. Then remove the lid and fluff it up with a fork. Now it's fluffy to perfection.

- Next, drain and squeeze out any excess water.
- Transfer quinoa into a larger size bowl and add the garlic, lemon juice, parsley, mint, tomatoes, green onions, and salt to let the bulgur continue to absorb the liquid.
- Remove from refrigerator and add the extra virgin olive oil.
- Next, add the cucumbers and chickpeas and toss well.
- Serve and enjoy.

Vegetable Stew

Servings: 2
Total time: 45 mins

Ingredients
- 2 cups cooked quinoa (1¾ cup of water for every cup of quinoa)
- 1 red bell pepper (seeded)
- 1 yellow bell pepper (sliced)
- 2 medium zucchini (chopped)
- 1 garlic (minced)
- 1 tbsp olive oil
- 2 sprigs of thyme
- 1 tbsp chili pepper sauce
- 1 tbsp tomato paste
- salt and pepper

Preparation
- In a medium size pot, bring to boil 1 ¾ cup of water to every cup of quinoa. (If there is too much water, it will go mushy. If too little, it will be too dry). Simmer for 15 minutes. Remove the pot

from the heat and let it sit covered for 10 minutes more. Then remove the lid and fluff it up with a fork. Now it's fluffy to perfection.

- Meanwhile, wash and chop the vegetables into small pieces. Pan-fry the vegetables in the grapeseed oil and garlic in a pan for about 5-8 minutes. The vegetables should still have some crunch.
- Once the quinoa is done cooking, add it to the pan with the vegetables and mix well. Finally, add the chili pepper sauce and tomato paste.
- Season with salt and pepper to taste. Mix well again.
- **Optional:** For variety, you can add pinto beans or black beans also to this recipe.

Vegetable Sushi Roll

Servings: 1
Total time: 50 mins

Ingredients
- 2 cups sushi rice (short grain white rice)
- ½ rice vinegar
- ½ avocado (slices)
- ¼ white sugar
- 2-4 nori sheets
- ½ tsp wasabi powder
- 3 tsp soy sauce (low sodium)
- 1½ carrot (cut into thin like sticks)
- 2 celery stalks – (thin sliced)
- 1 spring onion (diced)

Dipping sauce:
- Soy sauce
- Pickled ginger

Preparation

- Place the sushi rice in a strainer and rinse thoroughly with water. Then simmer the sushi rice in salted water with the lid closed on low heat for about 15 minutes. Switch off the stove and let the rice swell for another 5 minutes. Remove the lid, stir in the rice vinegar and sugar and allow the sushi rice to cool completely – set aside.
- Next, wash and peel the vegetables (cut into thin strips)
- Place the two sheets of nori, rough side up, on top of each other on the sushi mat with an overlap of about 2 cm. spread the rice evenly over the nori sheet a little more than halfway.
- Place on top of the rice with the vegetable slices and the avocado.
- Roll up carefully with the help of the sushi mat with slight pressure. Leave about 2 cm of nori sheet at the end, moisten the end with water and close the roll.
- Cut the roll in half and enjoy like a wrap with the soy sauce.
- Top with a small dab of wasabi and pickled ginger.

Tomato & Herb
"No EGG" Quiche

Servings: 1
Total time: 30 mins

Ingredients
For the dough:
- 3 ½ cups pastry flour or – gluten-free sorghum flour
- 1 ½ cups of butter
- ¾ cup of filtered water
- ½ tsp sea salt

Filling:
- 3 cups of cherry tomato(s)
- 2 silken firm tofu
- 2 tbsp olive oil
- 2 tbsp of cornstarch
- 1 teaspoon sea salt
- 1 cup spinach (chopped)
- Some freshly ground pepper
- 1 tsp fresh thyme

- 1 tsp fresh oregano
- ¼ cup of chives, fresh
- 3 tbsp basil, fresh

Preparation

- For the quiche dough, work all the ingredients into a smooth dough, cover and let rest in the fridge for 30 minutes.
- For the filling, wash the tomatoes, dry them well, cut them in half and set aside. Puree the silken tofu with the oil, cornstarch, salt and herbs spices to a creamy consistency. Wash the fresh herbs, shake them dry, chop finely and stir into the filling.
- Roll out the dough on a large piece of parchment paper to the size of a quiche pie plate plus the edge and slide it into the pie plate with the parchment paper. Press the dough into the mold and press the edges firmly as well.
- Preheat oven to 390 ° F for 10 minutes.
- Then spread the filling on the dough and cover the filling with the halved tomatoes, skin side down (this way, the water from the tomatoes does not soak the quiche.
- Bake the quiche in the hot oven for another 20 minutes. Then reduce the temperature to 350 °F and bake the quiche for another 15 minutes or until you see it golden and firm.
- Let the quiche rest for 10 minutes before slicing and then serve.
- Serve on romaine lettuce leaves and enjoy.

Cauliflower Steaks With Herbs & Spices

Servings: 4
Total time: 30 mins

Ingredients
- 1 head of cauliflower florets
- 2 cloves of garlic (mince)
- 2 tbsp of olive oil
- 1 tsp of chili pepper flakes
- 1 tsp of curry powder
- 2 juice of lemon
- 1 tbsp maple syrup
- pinch of sea salt

Preparation
- Preheat oven to 350 °F degrees
- Remove the outer leaves of any of the cauliflower, cut the cauliflower into thick slices and place into a medium size mixing bowl set aside. (Any leftover cauliflower pieces save for the next recipe)

- In a smaller mixing bowl, whisk together olive oil, maple syrup, garlic, salt, curry powder and lemon juice. Then pour the mixture over the cauliflower steaks. Toss and coat well.
- Place the cauliflower steaks on a flat baking tray and sprinkle on the chili peppers.
- Put coated cauliflower steaks into the oven for 10-15 minutes or until tender.
- Remove from the oven, and pour a bit of olive oil and lemon juice over the top for a zester taste.

Cauliflower
Garlic Hummus

Servings: 8
Total time: 30 mins

Ingredients
- 1 medium-head cauliflower
- ¼ cup hemp hearts
- 1 can of chickpeas (drained & rinsed)
- ¼ cup tahini paste
- 4 tablespoon olive oil (divided)
- 1-2 tbsp. fresh lemon juice
- 2-3 cloves garlic
- 1 teaspoon cumin
- ½ tsp. salt
- 2-4 tbsp. water

toppings (optional)
- olive oil
- fresh parsley
- cumin or paprika

Preparation

- Preheat the oven to 400 °F. Cut the cauliflower into small florets. Toss the cauliflower florets in 2 tablespoons of olive oil and spread evenly onto a large baking sheet. Bake for 20 minutes, occasionally stirring until the cauliflower is tender and cooked all the way through.
- Remove from the oven and transfer to a large food processor or high-speed blender. Add the remaining ingredients and blend until very smooth, scraping down the sides as needed. You will need to add 2-4 tablespoons of water to reach desired consistency. Add 1 tablespoon at a time once you have smooth hummus, taste and adjust seasonings.
- Serve with desired toppings and crackers, type pita bread, or vegetables.

Bok Choy
Miso Soup

Servings: 2
Total time: 10 mins

Ingredients
Miso Soup
- 1 tablespoon coconut or sesame oil
- ½ yellow onion, thinly sliced
- 2 garlic cloves, minced
- 1 tablespoon fresh ginger, peeled and minced
- 4 large bok choy leaves sliced thin
- 6 ounces tofu, cubed
- 4 cups vegetable broth
- 1 tbsp. yellow miso
- 1 large handful of spinach
- 2 green onions, thinly sliced

Preparation
- In a small soup pot, heat the coconut oil over medium heat. Add the onions and sauté until translucent and fragrant, about 8 minutes. Stir in the garlic and ginger and cook for another minute.

- Add the bok choy and tofu, stirring to coat. Pour in the vegetable broth and bring to a boil, then reduce heat and let simmer for 5 minutes, until bok choy has slightly wilted. Stir in the miso, spinach, and green onions and remove from heat.
- Serve immediately with hot chili sauce or sliced chili peppers and extra green onions.

Tasty No-Meat Tacos

Servings: 8-12 tacos
Total time: 45 mins

Ingredients
Taco Filling
- 1 package of meatless ground
- ½ can of black beans (drained and rinsed)
- ½ medium onion white or yellow (chopped)
- 1 tbsp. olive oil
- 1 tsp. crushed garlic
- ¼ tsp. chili pepper flakes
- ½ can of sweet corn (drained and rinsed)
- ½ cup of green pimento olives (chopped)
- 1 cup of shredded tex mex cheese.
- 2 medium tomatoes (chopped)
- salt and pepper to taste

Assembling:
- 2 cups shredded lettuce
- 2 medium avocados (mashed)

- 12-16 corn, wheat or cauliflower shells

Preparation
- If you're making these tacos with the premade meatless ground, it is a great start.
- Add the chopped onion to a pan along with the olive oil and crushed garlic, and sauté until the onions are softened. Add next the chili flakes and black beans and sauté with the onions and spices until heated through. If it's getting too dry in the pan, add a little water. Add salt and pepper to taste.
- Prepare your shredded Lettuce, tomatoes, olives, corn and mashed avocado.
- Assemble into the taco shells by adding to each some the cooked meatless ground, corn, olives, Lettuce, and tomatoes and top with the mashed avocado.

Cabbage And Potato Stew

Servings: 3
Total time: 50 mins

Ingredients
- ½ head white cabbage (chopped)
- 1 medium cooking onion
- 4 russet potato (peeled & cleaned)
- 1 tbsp, dijon mustard
- 1 liter vegetable broth
- 1 teaspoon cumin powder
- 1 pinch of sweet paprika powder
- 1 medium tomato (diced)
- salt and pepper
- 3 tbsp grapeseed oil

Preparation
- Remove the few outer leaves and center them from the cabbage. Cut the cabbage into slices.
- Remove the onion's skin and cut it into small pieces.

- Heat the vegetable oil in a pan or similar, sauté the onion and after a short time, add the cabbage. Season with cumin and paprika. When the cabbage has become soft, add the vegetable broth, and bring it to a boil. Then simmer on medium.
- In the meantime, peel and dice the potatoes. After about 20 minutes, add the potatoes, add chopped tomato to the stew and simmer for another 10 - 15 minutes.
- When everything is soft, add the mustard and season with salt and pepper as needed.

Onion-Cutting Tips:
- To prevent onion-induced tears
- Freeze the onion beforehand
- Soak the onion in cold water.
- Use a super-sharp knife
- Wear goggles! haha

Nutty Butter Spreads

Servings: 2-4
Total time: 20 mins

Ingredients
- 2 cups nut of choice: raw almonds, peanuts, macadamia cashews and pistachios
- ¼ tsp of pink salt or to taste
- add in options: cinnamon powder, maple syrup, monk fruit to taste

Preparation
- Put the nuts in a blender and process on high speed until creamy and smooth. Keep scraping down the sides frequently! The mixture starts to form a dry paste. And ball adds a bit of neutral oil, like grapeseed oil and resumes blending again.
- Add in your salt or sweetener of choice and continue blending.
- Scrap out of the blender and put it in a mixing bowl to cool before you put it into a glass jar.
- It can be stored in the refrigerator for 3-4 weeks.
- **Note:** Different types of nuts take longer to process due to the number of fatty acids. Almonds have less fat, so they take a little

more time in a food processor. If you make a lot of your own almond butter, investing in a high-speed blender or a Vitamix works extremely well.

- Cashews, pecans and peanuts have more fat, so they typically only take about 10 to 15 minutes to process in a food processor.

So Yummy

SNACK ATTACK RECIPES

Roasted Spicy Crunchy Chickpeas

Servings: 28
Total time: 35 mins

Ingredients
- 2 (14-ounce) cans of chickpeas, drained and rinsed
- 3 tablespoons nutritional yeast
- 2 tablespoons olive oil
- 2 teaspoons chili powder
- 1 teaspoon onion powder
- salt to taste

Preparation
- Preheat oven to 400 degrees F (200 degrees C).
- Mix chickpeas, nutritional yeast, olive oil, chili powder, onion powder, and salt together in a bowl until combined. Spread evenly on a rimmed baking sheet.
- Bake in the preheated oven, shaking the pan occasionally to re-distribute chickpeas, until crispy, 30 to 40 minutes.

Stuffed Avocado Boat

Servings: 15
Total time: 25 mins

Ingredients

- 2 avocados (halved and pitted)
- 8 cherry tomatoes (halved)
- 2 tbsp. red onions (finely chopped)
- ½ cup of canned black beans (rinsed)
- ½ english cucumber (cubed)
- ¼ cup cooked quinoa (1 ¾ cup of water for every cup of quinoa)
- ¼ of canned corn (rinsed)
- 2 tsp. fresh dill (finely chopped)
- 2 tbsp. extra-virgin olive oil
- 1 tbsp. lemon juice
- kosher salt as per taste
- freshly ground black pepper as per taste

Preparation

- Take a medium-sized bowl and toss the tomatoes, red onion, olives, dill, lemon juice, olive oil, and cucumber.

- Toss and season this mix all ingredients together; add the salt and pepper, as per your taste.
- Now, cut it in half & scoop out the flesh of each avocado.
- Leave ½ inch border so you can stuff it with the ingredients.
- Fill each of the avocado halves with the mixture you have already prepared.
- Serve the avocado immediately and enjoy.

NOTE: Incidentally, the small, black-purple avocados ("Hass" variety) work better than the large, green ones ("Fuertes" variety). The shell is thicker, harder and doesn't break as easily when spooned out as with the green ones. Fuertes, on the other hand, is better suited for peeling, i.e. for guacamole and salads.

Gourmet
Snow Balls

Servings: 7 balls
Total time: 20 mins

Ingredients
- 2 cups walnuts or other nut/seed of choice
- 1 cup shredded unsweetened coconut to roll finished
- 2 cups soft medjool dates, pitted
- ½ teaspoon sea salt
- 1 teaspoon vanilla extract

Preparation
- In a food processor or blender, process the walnuts
- Add in the dates, vanilla and sea salt and process again until a sticky, uniform batter is formed. (You can add a tablespoon of coconut oil, only if needed to help the mixture come together.) You don't want to over-process, or the batter will become oily, so process until crumbly but sticky when pressed between your fingers.

- Scoop the ingredients by heaping tablespoons, then roll between your hands to form balls. Roll in shredded coconut (chocolate and sprinkle with sesame seeds).
- Arrange them on a baking sheet lined with parchment paper, then place them in the fridge or freezer to set for at least 30 minutes before serving. Store the balls in a sealed container in the fridge for up to a week or in the freezer.

NOTE: Looks like gourmet truffles; you can also roll them in shredded coconut, sesame seeds or cocoa powder before chilling.

Pick Up & Go
Broccoli Vegetable Balls

Servings: 20 balls
Total time: 20 mins

Ingredients
- 2½ cups of raw broccoli florets
- 2½ cups of organic raw cashews
- ¼ cup of chopped red onion
- 1 cup red bell pepper (seeded and chopped)
- 2 cloves of garlic
- 1 tsp of avocado oil
- 1 chopped jalapeno
- ¼ cup of nutritional yeast or amino acids
- ½ tsp of fresh ground black pepper
- ½ tsp of sea salt

Preparation
- Put all ingredients, broccoli, chopped pepper and cashew, in a food processor or high-speed blender or pulse to chop, but do not overdo it.
- Add all remaining ingredients and pulse blend until everything is well combined and has a slightly wet and crumbly consistency.
- Scoop out, and shape into small balls – place in the refrigerator until firm.

Coconut Milk Rice With Caramelized Bananas

Servings: 4
Total time: 35 mins

Ingredients
- 3 cups of coconut milk
- ½ cup basmati rice
- ½ cup of raw sugar
- 2 pinches salt
- 1 cinnamon stick
- 1 cup raw sugar
- 2 tbsp lemon juice
- 2 bananas, sliced
- 4 tbsp almond slices
- 3 tbsp unsalted raw pistachios (shell removed)

Preparation
- Bring the water with all the ingredients up to and including the cinnamon stick to a boil, reduce the heat, and simmer over low

heat for approx. 20 minutes, occasionally stirring, to a thick but still moist porridge. Remove the cinnamon stick.

- Bring the sugar and water to a boil without stirring. Reduce the heat and simmer, rocking the pan from time to time until a light brown caramel is obtained. Remove the pan from the plate. Add the lemon juice, cover and simmer the caramel until it has dissolved.
- Add the bananas, and simmer for approx. 1 min. Spread the bananas on the rice pudding. Scatter the almonds and pistachios and garnish the rice pudding.

Fabulous Baked Falafel

Servings: 20
Total time: 40 mins

Ingredients
- 1 cup of dry chickpea (soak overnight)
- 1 large yellow onion (chopped)
- 2 cloves garlic (minced)
- 1 bunch parsley = approximately 1 cup (finely chopped)
- 1 bunch cilantro = approximately 1 cup (finely chopped)
- pinch of sea salt
- 1 tsp cardamom powder
- ¼ cup of chickpea flour
- ½ tsp of baking soda
- 1-2 tbsp of avocado oil

Tzatziki Sauce
- ½ english cucumber (grated)
- 1 ½ cups of use greek yogurt
- ¼ cup of dill (chopped)

- 2 garlic cloves
- 1 tbsp of extra virgin olive oil
- 2 tbsp of freshly squeezed lemon juice
- pinch of sea salt to taste
- put all ingredients in a food processor or blender
- blend until well combined. serve immediately.

Preparation

- For the delicious falafel, soak the chickpeas in plenty of water (2 inches above the chickpeas) the day before. Drain the water the next day.
- Preheat oven to 375 ° F – Spray a baking tray with cooking oil.
- Then wash the cilantro and parsley, and finely peel and finely dice the garlic and onion and add to the food processor or blender.
- Then add the uncooked chickpeas, salt, pepper, cumin, and cardamom and continue processing and puree everything finely.
- Scoop out and transfer the mixture to a mixing bowl and add the chickpea flour and baking soda. Mix and cover. Place in the refrigerator for 1 hour.
- Next, remove the mixture from the fridge with slightly damp hands, scoop and flatten the mixture into small patties. If the mixture is too wet, add more chickpea flour, and if too dry, add some water or lemon juice. Place on a baking tray.
- Bake the falafel patties for 10-12 minutes, flip the patties and bake for another 10-12 minutes or until the mixture is golden brown and cooked thoroughly.

Guacamole With
SUNDRIED Tomato On Toast

Servings: 1-2
Total time: 7 mins

Ingredients
- 2 slices of bread of choice
- ½ avocado(s) (mashed)
- 5 sundried tomatoes (finely chopped)
- ½ of a squeeze of lime juice
- 1 splash of olive oil
- 1 clove of garlic (minced)
- 1 sprout (alfalfa or beetroot sprouts)
- leaf or boston lettuce
- sea salt and fresh ground pepper

Preparation
- First, make guacamole: Mash the avocado in a mixing bowl with a fork. Add salt, pepper, finely chopped (fresh) garlic, a dash of olive oil and a squeeze of lime juice.
- Use the toasted bread of your choice and place the sundried tomatoes on top of the sandwich.
- Optionally: add the alfalfa or beetroot sprouts for garnish.

Fruit
Crumble Bars

Servings: 9
Total time: 55 mins

Ingredients
For the filling
- 4 cups fresh fruit (mixed berries)
- ½ cup sugar
- 1 tbsp orange zest
- 1 tsp vanilla extract
- 3 tbsp chia seeds

For the crumble
- 1 ½ cups rolled oats
- 2 cups regular flour or (bob's red mill all purpose gluten free flour)
- 1 cup brown sugar
- ½ tsp salt
- 1 cup vegan butter (like earth balance), melted

Preparation
- Begin by making the filling. Over medium heat, bring the mixed fruit, which includes raspberries and sugar, to a boil. Let the

mixture cook until mostly all the rhubarb has lost its shape, about 15 minutes.

- Take the fruit mixture off the heat and stir in the orange zest, vanilla, and chia seeds.
- While the filling is cooling (about 15 minutes), preheat the oven to 350 degrees Fahrenheit and line a 9 x 9-inch pan with parchment paper.
- Mix together the flour, oats, brown sugar, and salt in a medium-sized mixing bowl.
- Add the melted butter to the flour and oat mixture and mix well.
- Take 2/3 of the crumble and press it down into the prepared pan. Then spread the fruit mixture on top. Finally, place the remaining crumble on top of the filling.
- Bake in the oven for 40 minutes. Let cool completely before cutting into slices.

Meatless
Spicy Jerky

Servings: 2
Total time: 45 mins

Ingredients
- 2 cups dry soy curls
- 2 cups boiling water
- 1 tbsp olive oil
- 2 tbsp tamari
- 2 tbsp nutritional yeast
- 1 tbsp maple syrup
- 2 tsp liquid smoke
- ¾ tsp garlic powder
- ½ tsp onion powder
- ¾ tsp smoked paprika (optional)

Preparation
- Prepare the soy curls by covering them with boiling water. Let rehydrate for 2 minutes. Then drain them and rinse them well. Squeeze out as much water as you can.
- Combine the rest of the ingredients in a small bowl.

- Preheat the oven to 300 degrees Fahrenheit and line a baking sheet with parchment paper.
- In a medium-sized bowl, combine the soy curls with the sauce. Let sit while the oven preheats.
- When the oven is ready, place the soy curls on the baking sheet, and spread them out evenly. The soy curls should have mostly been absorbed, but if they didn't - make sure you don't get that extra liquid onto the baking sheet, or these won't dry out the way they should.
- Bake for 30 minutes, then toss. Bake for another 15 - 30 minutes. Important note: if the soy curls were squeezed really well and soaked up all the marinade, no problem, they'll likely only need another 15 minutes; otherwise, they'll get crunchy. If they were a little "wetter", the soy curls would take longer to dehydrate. You don't want them crispy or too soft, so keep an eye on them in the last 15 - 30 minutes of baking.
- Let the soy curls cool on the baking sheet. When they're cooled, you can store them in a zip-lock bag or in a glass-sealable container. You can freeze them as well.

So Yummy
DESSERT
RECIPES

—◆—

Simple Chocolate Cake With Fruit Sauce (Gluten Free)

Servings: 1
Total time: 45 mins

Ingredients
- 1 cup oat flour
- ¼ cup of cocoa baking powder
- ¾ cup of raw sugar
- ½ pack baking powder
- 1 cup of filtered water
- 3 ½ ounces of oil (sunflower or olive oil)

Preparation

- Preheat to 350 °F and bake for about 35 minutes on the middle rack.
- Mix the solid and wet ingredients separately.
- Then mix everything together. Grease a round spring from the pan and pour in the batter.
- Remove when the cake is cooled.

Fruit Sauce

- 2 cups of fruit (raspberry peaches, pineapple
- ½ cup agave syrup
- Place the ingredients into a high-speed blender until smooth consistency.
- Use immediately or store in the refrigerator for 3-4 days.

No Bake - ZESTY
Lemon Mini Squares

Servings: 4+
Total time: 20 mins

Ingredients
No Bake Crust:
- 3 cups of nuts, walnuts or almonds (soak)
- 3 cups of pitted medjool dates (soak)
- 1 tbsp of pure vanilla
- 1-2 tbsp of agave syrup
- ¼ tsp sea salt

Key Lime Pie Filling:
- 1 ¼ cups whole cashews
- ¼ cup full-fat coconut milk
- ¼ – ½ cup lemon juice (plus more to taste)

- ¼ of lemon zest
- 1 tablespoon lime zest
- ¼ cup maple syrup (plus more to taste)
- 1 teaspoon vanilla extract
- 2 tablespoons coconut oil

Preparation

- Place the nuts and salt into a food processor with a pulse setting, leaving it a bit chunky.
- Add dates and vanilla and process until it binds together and dates form a cake batter. Add some of the date water if it gets too clumpy.
- Test the batter to see if it holds together; if not, add some more dates.
- Press the dough into an 8×8 baking pan lined with parchment paper. Put the crust in the fridge or freezer while you prepare the key lime filling.

Lemon Filling Preparation

- Add the soaked cashews, lime juice, lime zest, maple syrup, coconut oil, coconut milk, and vanilla extract to your food process or high-powered blender. Blend the filling until silky smooth, and creamy.
- Give the filling a taste and adjust the level of sweetness or tartness to your taste. You can add more maple syrup or add more lime juice to suit your taste buds.
- Pour the key lime filling over the prepared crust. Freeze the bars overnight or until completely solid.
- When you are ready to serve, remove the bars from the freezer and use a sharp knife to slice the bars into 9 or 16 pieces.
- **Optional:** Top with lemon zest and enjoy!

No-Bake Blueberry Cheese-Like Cake

Servings: 12
Total time: 2 hours +

Ingredients
Crust:
- 1 cup rolled oats (gluten-free, if needed)
- ¼ cup raw almonds
- 2 tablespoons coconut sugar
- 2 tablespoons unsweetened shredded coconut
- 2 tablespoons melted coconut oil

Filling:
- 1 ½ cups raw blanched almonds (soaked)
- 1 ½ cups fresh or frozen blueberries
- ¼ cup lemon juice
- ¼ cup + 2 tablespoons pure maple syrup
- ¼ cup coconut oil
- 1 teaspoon vanilla extract

Preparation
Crust:

- Add the rolled oats, almonds, and coconut sugar to a food processor or a high-speed blender.
- Blend until the almonds and oats have broken down.
- Add the shredded coconut and the coconut oil.
- Pulse until everything has combined.
- Divide the mixture evenly between 12 muffin tin cups and press it down until it is packed well.
- Place the muffin tin in the freezer for the bases to firm up. Chill for at least 20 minutes.

Filling:
- Add the almonds, blueberries, lemon juice, maple syrup, coconut oil, and vanilla to a high-speed blender.
- Blend until the mixture is smooth and creamy. You may need to use your blender's tamper to keep it going.
- Remove the chilled "base" from the freezer and divide the cheesecake mixture evenly between the 12 muffin cups. Smooth out the tops and place them back in the freezer for at least 2 hours for them to firm up.
- Remove from freezer ½ hour before serving so they can thaw a bit. Garnish and serve.
- Store uneaten cheesecakes in the freezer in an airtight container or share them with friends. Enjoy!

Simple Homemade Kiwi Sorbet

Servings: 3-4
Total time: 2 hours +

Ingredients
- 5 kiwi fruit (skin removed & sliced)
- 1 tbsp of lime juice
- ¼ cup of raw sugar

Preparation
- Peel the kiwi fruit, and cut it into slices. Place in the freezer for an hour or so.
- Once frozen, put into a food processor or high-speed blender and add lime juice and sugar. Pulse until it reaches the desired sorbet consistency.
- Serve immediately or freeze for later.

Super Delish Chocolate Banana Chia Pudding

Servings: 4
Total time: 6 hours

Ingredients
- 6 medjool dates (pits removed)
- ¼ cup unsweetened cocoa powder
- ½ cup of oat milk
- 1 teaspoon vanilla extract
- ½ cup filtered water
- ¼ cup chia seeds (the perfect ratio – (¼ cup chia to 1 cup liquid)

Preparation
- Soak dates in water for 30 minutes to soften them up.
- Add dates, bananas, cocoa powder, coconut milk, vanilla, and water to a blender.
- Blend until smooth.
- Pour the mixture into a large mixing bowl.
- Stir in chia seeds.
- Cover and refrigerate for a few hours or overnight so it can set.

- **Optional:** Garnish with sliced almonds, raspberries or blueberries.

Apple Crumble

Servings: 6
Total time: 45 mins

Ingredients

Apple Layer:

- 4 cups tart apples (peeled, cored and sliced, use granny smith or honey crisp or a combination of both.
- 1 tablespoon coconut sugar (or brown sugar)
- 2 tablespoons pure maple syrup
- 2 teaspoons fresh lemon juice
- 2 teaspoons arrowroot starch (cornstarch can also be used)
- 1 teaspoon ground cinnamon
- ¼ teaspoon ground nutmeg
- ¼ teaspoon ground ginger
- ¼ teaspoon salt

Crunchy Topping:

- 1 ¼ cups rolled oats
- ½ cup oat flour
- ¼ cup coconut sugar (or brown sugar)

- ¼ teaspoon ground cinnamon
- ¼ cup soft coconut oil + a little extra for greasing baking dish or ramekins
- **Note:** top the topping with vanilla frozen yogurt

Preparation
- Preheat oven to 350° F (177° C).
- Lightly grease the bottom and sides of the 8 x 8 baking dish (grease with coconut oil)
- Peel, quarter, and slice apples.
- Add apples, coconut sugar, maple syrup, lemon juice, arrowroot starch, cinnamon, nutmeg, ginger, and salt to a bowl. Stir until combined.
- Add apples to an 8 x 8 baking dish and spread, so you have an even layer. Set aside.
- Add rolled oats, oat flour, coconut sugar, and cinnamon to a bowl and whisk until combined.
- Add coconut oil to the oat mixture and mix until combined and crumbly.
- Add all of the oat mixtures to the top of the apple mixture and spread to make an even, loose layer (don't pack it down).
- If using individual ramekins, divide the oat mixture evenly among the ramekins by adding to the top of the apples (don't pack it down).
- If using an 8 x 8 dish, bake for 45 minutes until the fruit is bubbling and the top is golden.
- If using ramekins for 30-35 minutes until the fruit is bubbling and the top is golden.
- Cool before serving, and still warm.
- Top with vanilla yogurt or coconut whip cream.

Watermelon Popsicle

Servings: 8
Total time: 5 hours 40 mins

Ingredients
- 650 g watermelon
- 12 leaves peppermint
- 1 tbsp lemon juice

Preparation
- Remove the skin of the watermelon, cut it into pieces, and put it into a blender.
- Add peppermint leaves and puree them together. Pour into the ice cream molds and freeze for approx. 4 hours.

Potato Pancakes
Without Eggs

Servings: 4
Total time: 30 mins

Ingredients
- 6-7 yukon gold (peeled & grated)
- 5 tsp flour
- 1 medium onion
- 1 tsp salt
- 5 tsp extra olive oil

Preparation
- First, peel the potatoes, then grate them finely and then salt them. This will remove the starch from the potatoes. Now let the mixture stand for 2-3 minutes.
- Now peel the onions and finely grate them.
- Then squeeze the potato mixture firmly with your hands and collect the potato water in a bowl.
- Now mix the grated onion and the remaining salt into the potato mixture.

- To bind together, add 5 tablespoons of the previously reserved potato water to the flour and mix. Add this mixture to the remaining potato mixture and mix well again.
- Heat the oil in a pan and fry the pancakes on both sides evenly until golden and crispy.

General Tao Tofu, Broccoli & Rice

Servings: 4-6
Total time: 40 mins

Ingredients
General TaoTofu
- 1 (12oz) block of extra firm tofu
- 2 tablespoons cornstarch
- 1 teaspoon grated fresh ginger
- 3 cloves garlic (pressed or minced)
- 2 tablespoons tamari or soy sauce
- 2 tablespoons oil

Veggie & Rice
- 2 teaspoons grated fresh ginger
- 3 cloves garlic (pressed or minced)
- 2 tablespoons toasted sesame or regular oil
- 1 large head of broccoli cut into florets (approximately 4 cups)
- 2 stems of green onion (chopped)
- ¼ cup low sodium tamari or soy sauce

- 4 cups cooked jasmine rice (perfect ratio for slightly firmer rice - 1 part water to 2/3 rice or softer rice - 2 parts water to 1 part rice)

Preparation
Prepare the tofu:
- Slice the pressed block of tofu into bite-sized cubes and toss in a bowl with cornstarch.
- Whisk together 1 teaspoon of grated ginger, 3 cloves of pressed or minced garlic, and 2 tablespoons of tamari or soy sauce. Set aside.
- Heat a large metal or cast-iron skillet over medium heat.
- Once the skillet is hot, add 2 tablespoons of oil and swirl to coat.
- Place all pieces of tofu in the pan and fry. Once golden brown on 1 side, flip all the pieces, so the other sides get golden brown, as well.
- Once both sides are crispy and golden brown, remove any excess oil from the pan and add the ginger/garlic/soy mixture.
- Mix around with a spoon until all tofu pieces are coated.
- Remove tofu from the skillet and place in a bowl. Set aside.

Prepare vegetables and rice:
- Heat a large skillet on medium-high heat.
- Once it's hot, add 2 tablespoons of sesame seed oil and swirl to coat.
- Add the 2 teaspoons of grated ginger and minced garlic and fry for a minute.
- Add the broccoli and stir fry till the broccoli becomes a bright green color.
- Add the 4 tablespoons of tamari or soy sauce and stir.
- Add the green onion and stir fry for another 2 minutes.
- Add the cooked tofu. Mix again to evenly distribute the tofu pieces.
- Top over cooked rice. Enjoy this is So Yummy!

So Yummy
DINNER RECIPES

Kale Salad With Fennel & Zesty Dressing

Servings: 15
Total time: 10 mins

Ingredients
- 2 cups kale (chopped)
- ½ cup fennel (sliced)
- 1-2 tsp olive oil
- ¼ cup raw pumpkin seeds
- ¼ cup red sliced onion
- ¼ cup cranberries
- pinch of celtic salt

Zesty Dressing:
- 2 tbsp fresh lemon juice
- ¼ cup olive oil
- 1 clove minced garlic
- ¼ of chopped dill
- 2 tbsp red wine vinegar
- 1 tbsp dijon mustard

- 1 tsp maple syrup

Preparation
- Make your dressing by mixing all the ingredients listed above and place in a glass jar. Shake well and adjust the taste if needed.
- In a mixing bowl, place the chopped kale, then massage with lemon and salt until wilted - then wash off the salt and pat dry). Add the onion, pumpkin seeds, fennel, and cranberries and sprinkle a pinch of salt. Pour over the dressing, toss and coat well.
- Place in the refrigerator for about an hour and then serve.

Mediterranean Salad

Servings: 4-6
Total time: 60 mins

Ingredients
- 3 cups of couscous (perfect ratio 1 ¼ of water or broth to 1 cup of couscous)
- 1 can chickpeas (drained & rinsed)
- 3 zucchinis (diced)
- 5 green onions (chopped)
- 1 red bell pepper (chopped & seeded)
- 1 yellow bell pepper (chopped & seeded)
- ½ cup of sesame seeds

Lemon Dressing
- ½ cup of extra virgin olive oil
- 1 juice of lemon
- 4 cloves of garlic (minced or pressed)

Preparation

- Add couscous into a pot of water, stir until well combined & bring to a boil. Reduce heat and cover. Fluff with a fork. When it's done, set it to the side.
- Then add the vegetables and chickpea to the couscous.
- In a jar, make the dressing and shake well.
- Pour the dressing over the couscous vegetable mixture.
- Season with sea salt and fresh ground pepper.

No-Meat
No Noodle Lasagna

Servings: 6
Total time: 25

Ingredients
- 1 package of vegan ground meat

Cheeze Like Ingredients:
- 2 tbsp of fresh lemon juice
- 1 cup fresh cashew nuts
- 1 tbsp of fresh thyme
- pinch of sea salt and pepper
- ¾ cup almond milk or cashew milk (not flavored)
- 2 tbsp nutritional yeast

Tomato Sauce Ingredients:
- 2 tbsp extra-virgin olive oil
- 4 tbsp filtered water
- 1 tbsp chopped fresh basil
- ⅓ cup sun-dried tomatoes packed in olive oil
- 7 medium sized tomatoes

- 3 garlic cloves (finely chopped or minced)
- 1 tbsp fresh lemon juice

Vegetable Layers:
- a handful of fresh spinach
- 2 length sliced zucchinis

Preparation
- Soak the cashew nuts in water for 1 hour (minimum) for the cheese-like taste.
- **Prepare the Tomato Sauce:** Drain the oil from the sundried tomatoes before transferring it to the blender. Add the olive oil, tomatoes, filtered water, basil, garlic and lemon juice. Pulse till all ingredients are combined and mildly textured. Pour it into a bowl; cover and refrigerate till you are ready to assemble the lasagna. Clean your blender for the next step.
- **Prepare the Cheese Sauce:** Drain the water from the soaked cashew and move it to the cleaned blender. Add the lemon juice, thyme, almond milk, sea salt and pepper, and nutritional yeast. Blend all ingredients till a smooth, silky sauce is gotten. Pour into a bowl, cover and refrigerate till you are ready to assemble the lasagna. Clean the blender for the next step.
- **Prepare the vegetables:** Slice your zucchinis into long strips using your vegetable slicer. as thin as you can. Wash the spinach and basil leaves.
- Pan-fry the vegan meat with some onions.
- To assemble the layers like a lasagna in a rectangle baking dish by starting with the sauce and then the zucchini slices; add the vegan meat, spinach, tomato sauce, and cheese mixture. Repeat the layer and garnish with fresh basil leaves and thyme.

Cauliflower Rice Bolognese With Lentils

Servings: 4
Total time: 20 mins

Ingredients
- 1 head cauliflower (finely chopped – minced)
- 1 red onion (finely chopped)
- 3 cloves of garlic (minced)
- 1 stalk of celery
- 2 cans of crushed tomatoes
- 3 tbsp tomato paste
- 10 cherry tomatoes (cut in half)
- 200 ml vegetable broth
- 1 tsp salt
- ½ tsp pepper
- ½ tsp basil
- ½ tsp thyme
- 1 can of lentils (drained and rinsed)
- 2 tbsp nutritional yeast flakes (as topping – tastes like cheese)

Preparation

- Wash cauliflower, separate florets and put into a food processor until it becomes cauliflower rice.
- Peel or wash other vegetables and chop them into small pieces.
- In a saucepan, sauté the onion and garlic in a sip of vegetable stock until translucent.
- After a few minutes, add diced celery and cauliflower, sauté for 5 minutes over medium heat and add the herbs.
- Then add chopped plum tomatoes (fresh or canned) and fill with vegetable broth until the ingredients are just covered.
- Add the lentils to the sauce.
- Season and simmer for another 5 minutes.
- **Optionally:** sprinkle with nutritional yeast flakes.

An Autumn Delight - Red Cabbage, Carrot & Apple Slaw

Servings: 4
Total time: 20 mins

Ingredients
- 1 medium red cabbage (thinly sliced)
- 2 crisp apples cored (peeled and julienne sliced)
- 2 medium carrots (peeled & julienne sliced)
- 1 tbsp raw apple cider vinegar
- 1 juice of fresh lemon
- ¼ cup of extra virgin oil
- 1 tsp of maple syrup
- 1 tsp of dijon mustard
- pinch of sea salt
- fresh tarragon to garnish

Preparation
- Add the slices of cabbage, carrot, and apple together in a mixing bowl.

- In another bowl, add maple syrup, sea salt, apple vinegar, and olive oil and whisk together to combine.
- Pour the above mixture over the Slaw and mix and toss well until all ingredients are well coated.
- The zest and flavor are so tasty if refrigerated for a minimum of 1 hour before serving.

Green Pesto With Zucchini Noodles

Servings: 2
Total time: 20 mins

Ingredients

Pesto Ingredients

- 2 cups of chopped basil
- ¼ cup of crushed pecans
- add 2 tbsp of raw sesame seeds
- use 1 tbsp of sesame tahini
- add 1 minced garlic clove
- add 2 tbsp of extra-virgin olive oil
- add a half tsp of lemon juice
- u¼ tsp of himalayan salt
- 4 cherry tomatoes (cut in half)

Zucchini Noodles

- 2-3 zucchinis (spiralized)

Preparation

- Put all the ingredients into either the food processor or high-speed blender, and blend until smooth.
- Spiralize the zucchini and mix thoroughly with the pesto mixture.
- Add in cherry tomatoes at the end.

No Meat Burgers
With Spicy Guacamole

Servings: 2
Total time: 30 mins

Ingredients
- 4 portobello mushrooms – cleaned and stem cut off

Spicy Guacamole
- ½ cup of lemon juice
- 1-2 tsp of coconut aminos
- 2 of cloves of garlic
- 1 finely chopped green onion
- 2 avocados (pitted)
- 1 red bell pepper (seeded and chopped)
- 1 shallot or ½ medium onion
- 2/3 cup of sun-dried tomatoes (soak until soft)
- 2-4 tbsp of amino acids
- 1 jalapeño (seeded & chopped)
- ½ tsp of chili pepper flakes
- cheeze like sauce

- 2 cup of your favorite nut or seed (almonds, cashew, brazil nuts, pumpkin sees or sunflower seeds)
- 1 tsp of chopped garlic
- ½ tsp of salt
- juice of 2 lemons
- ¼ cup of water is needed
- put garlic and salt into a food processor. next add the nuts of seeds and lemon juice and continue to blend. add water if needed.
- **NOTE:** keeps in refrigerator for 5 days.

Preparation
- Prepare the mushroom wash and clean and stem cut off. – pour some amino acids into the bottom cap, then set aside.
- Preheat oven to 350° F and place portobello mushroom caps on the baking tray bottom up. Bake until the mushroom is slightly cooked.
- Blend all ingredients for the guacamole in a food processor or high-speed blender until it becomes smooth and creamy.
- Spread the Spicy Guacamole filling over one grilled mushroom and use one mushroom cap to top like a bun. Fill the inside with cashew cheese sauce and mix greens and lettuce.
- Enjoy this "So Yummy" recipe!

Quick Easy Creamy
Miso Soup With Mushrooms

Servings: 6
Total time: 35 mins

Ingredients
Soup Base
- 6 cups water
- ¼ cup organic miso, yellow or white
- ½ cup hemp hearts (or pine nuts)
- ½ cup raw cashews (soaked)
- 1 tablespoon pure maple syrup
- 1 tablespoon dulse flakes or crushed dried wakame (optional)
- himalayan salt & pepper to taste

Mushroom Mixture
- 1 cup shiitakes, fresh (sliced)
- ½ cup baby cremini mushrooms (sliced)
- 2 tablespoons sesame oil or vegetable broth/water
- 2 tablespoons soy sauce, nama shoyu or coconut aminos
- juice of 1 – 2 medium lemons or 2 – 3 small limes
- 1 teaspoon red pepper flakes, adjust to your liking

Optional Garnish
- ¼ cup wakame or dulse
- scallions, sliced
- shallots, finely diced.

Preparation
- **Marinate Mushrooms:** In a medium size mixing bowl, combine the mushrooms with olive oil or broth, tamari, lemon/lime juice and red pepper flakes. Allow marinating for at least 30 minutes, stirring occasionally.
- **Soup Base:** In your blender, place the water, miso, hemp hearts, cashews, and maple syrup/agave, and blend until smooth. Taste for flavor, adding salt & pepper as needed. It will have some froth on top, and you can either leave it or scoop it off. I scooped most of it off. Add wakame/dulse, and let them absorb the soup.
- **Combine:** Once mushrooms are ready, add the mushroom mix to the blended soup and give a good stir.
- Serve as is or garnish with scallions. Also, feel free to warm it slightly before serving; place soup in a medium/large pot over medium heat, and heat until just warm.

Warm Up With A
Sweet Pepper Pistachio Soup

Servings: 4
Total time: 25 mins

Ingredients
Soup Base
- 3 cups vegetable broth
- 1½ cup filtered water
- 1 can of crushed tomatoes
- 1 tbsp extra virgin olive oil
- 2 large red bell peppers (seeded & chopped)
- 2 shallots (diced)
- 4 stalks of celery (chopped)
- 2 carrots (peeled & chopped)
- ½ tsp of chili pepper flakes
- ½ tsp fresh black pepper
- 2 cloves of garlic (minced)
- ¼ cup of cilantro or basil (finely chopped)
- 1 tbsp of fresh thyme
- 3 tbsp of fresh basil
- ¼ cup of raw shelled pistachios (shelled & soaked)

- ¼ cup finely chopped flat-leaf parsley (garnish)
- 1 tbsp of coconut aminos
- **optional:** ¼ cup of plain greek yogurt

Preparation
- In a large saucepan, heat oil and keep on medium heat. Add shallots, chili peppers, carrots, celery, and a pinch of salt and cook until soft.
- In a food processor, add step 1 and puree with the canned tomatoes, peppers, coconut aminos, vegetable broth and pistachios, basil or cilantro, and thyme. Blend until well combined.
- Remove liquid ingredients from the blender and pour into a medium-large size pot. Bring to boil the ingredients, then reduce heat and simmer for 30 min. Turn off the heat and stir in the yogurt if desired.
- Top the soup with some greek yogurt, drizzled olive oil and freshly ground pepper and parsley before serving.
- **Note:** Enjoy the soup immediately or refrigerate it till the next day as it will taste even better.

Vegetable Chili Carne

Servings: 4
Total time: 1 hour

Ingredients
- 5 carrots (peeled and chopped)
- 1 jalapeño pepper (seeded & diced)
- 1 yellow and 1 red bell pepper
- 2 tbsp of fresh parsley
- ½ tsp of chili pepper flakes
- 1 cup vegetable soup broth
- 1 cup filtered water
- 1 tbsp of virgin olive oil
- 2 cups of medium size tomatoes (chopped)
- 2 tsp tomato paste
- 2 stalks of celery
- 1 can of corn (drained & rinsed)
- 1 can of red or white kidney beans (drained and rinsed)
- 2 cloves of garlic (minced)
- 1 large yellow onion (chopped)

- salt & fresh ground pepper to taste

Preparation
- Using a vegetable peeler, clean and peel the carrots, then chop. Peel onion and garlic and finely chop.
- Take the beans and corn out of the can and rinse with clear water and drain.
- Wash the peppers, remove the seeds & cut them into small cubes.
- Now heat the oil in a saucepan; first, fry the onion with the garlic until golden. Add the carrots, peppers, jalapeño and celery and let it get slightly soft; stir continually.
- Next, add tomatoes and top up with the vegetable mixture. Finally, add the tomato paste and let it simmer for about 20 minutes on low heat.
- Meanwhile, finely chop the parsley and add chili flakes
- Just before the end of the cooking time, add the beans, corn, and parsley to the sauce pot. Season with salt and cayenne pepper to taste.
- Garnish with finely chopped parsley and season to taste.

Any Green Veggies & Peanut Soup

Servings: 4
Total time: 20 mins

Ingredients
- ½ cup raw peanuts or roasted peanuts (shelled)
- ½ cup water
- 1 cup broccoli, chopped
- 1 cup spinach
- 1 stalk of leek, sliced
- 1 garlic clove, chopped
- 1 tsp ginger, grated
- ¼ cup basil
- 1 chili pepper (seeded) and chopped
- 1 juice of fresh lemon
- pinch of black and white pepper
- pinch of sea salt

Preparation

- Blend the peanuts to a fine powder if possible
- Add water and blend again.
- Next, add the rest of the ingredients, and continue to add water until desired consistency is achieved.
- Flavors with whatever toppings you like, such as fresh herbs, nuts, croutons or seeds.
- **Note:** Many have enjoyed this easy-to-make Green Soup. This is truly a budget-friendly recipe; keep it in your memory. Just throw some peanuts in a blender, add water, and whatever green vegetables you have available or the ones suggested. Blend and serve.

Kung Pao Tofu With Green Onions & Broccoli

Servings: 4
Total time: 20 mins

Ingredients

Tofu

- 16 oz. extra-firm tofu, cut into 1" cubes
- 2 tbsp. soy sauce
- 2 tbsp. toasted sesame oil
- 2 tsp. cornstarch

Kung Pao Sauce

- ⅓ cup vegetable broth
- ¼ cup soy sauce (low sodium)
- 1-inch fresh ginger (grated)
- 2 cloves garlic, minced
- 1 tbsp. maple syrup

- 1 ½ tsp. cornstarch

Vegetables
- 2 tbsp. sesame oil
- 1 red pepper (seeded & sliced)
- 1 yellow pepper (seeded & slice)
- 3 green onions (chopped)
- 8-12 broccoli florets
- **optional:** ¼ cup raw cashews

Preparation
- Begin by making the tofu. Cut the tofu into 1" cubes and place in a large zip lock bag. Whisk together the soy sauce, sesame oil, and cornstarch until the cornstarch has dissolved. Pour the sauce over the tofu and let it marinate for 10 minutes while you prepare everything else.
- Whisk together the ingredients for the Kung Pao sauce and set aside.
- Heat a large skillet or wok over medium-high heat. Add 2 tablespoons of sesame oil. Once the oil is hot, add the marinated tofu, along with the extra marinade. Stir fry the tofu for 5-7 minutes, occasionally stirring, until the tofu begins to brown. Remove from heat and transfer the tofu into a small bowl.
- Add the remaining sesame oil to the pan. Once the oil is hot, add the red & yellow bell peppers, broccoli, and green onions. Sauté for 3-4 minutes until the vegetables are tender. Add the marinated sauce to the pan and bring to a boil, stirring constantly. Once the sauce begins to thicken, return to tofu to the pan and stir-fry it along with the vegetables for 2-3 more minutes.
- Garnish and add in some cashews.
- Remove from heat and serve immediately with steamed rice.

Greek Style Lemon Potatoes

Servings: 8
Total time: 20 mins

Ingredients

- 2 lbs. yukon baby potatoes (cut in half)
- 1 ½ cup of chicken broth (low sodium)
- 3 tbsp olive oil
- 1 tsp dried thyme leaves
- ½ tsp dry oregano
- ⅓ cup of fresh lemon juice
- 5 cloves of garlic (minced)
- ½ tsp of sea salt

Preparation

- Preheat oven to 390 ° F
- Peel and cut potatoes and place in roasting pan. Add all ingredients and toss well. Toss potatoes in vegetable broth, olive oil, garlic, lemon, thyme, oregano and salt.

- Roast for 25-30 minutes until all liquid is absorbed. Turn over 2 times during that time until the potatoes are golden and crispy looking. Toss again in the left-over marinate, check and see if it needs more baking time.
- Finally, turn off the oven and let it sit in the juices and then serve it up.
- Garnish with fresh thyme and dig in!

No-Meat
Meat Balls

Servings: 4
Total time: 1 hour

Ingredients

- 2 cups peeled and diced eggplant
- 1 cup of canned pinto beans (drained & rinsed)
- 1 cup cremini mushrooms (cleaned & chopped)
- 1 ½ cups breadcrumbs (homemade or bought)
- 1 cup walnuts
- 2 tbsp flat leaf parsley (minced)
- 1 tbsp of soy sauce (low sodium)
- 1 tsp nutritional yeast
- 1 tbsp of tomato paste
- 2 tsp italian herb seasoning
- 1 tsp garlic powder
- salt & pepper to taste

Preparation

- Preheat oven to 350 ° F Place beans and eggplant on a lined baking sheet and bake for 10-15 minutes.
- Meanwhile, pulse the walnuts and herbs in a food processor until nearly a flour-like texture. Add the mushrooms, breadcrumbs, pinto beans and eggplant. Pulse until well combined but still with some texture remaining.
- Form the mixture into balls and place them on a lined baking sheet. Bake for 30-35 minutes or until the outside is firm and the inside is tender. Let cool for 10 minutes before serving.
- Serve on a bed of rice, quinoa or spiralized zucchini. Super yummy!

Creamy Cabbage Broccoli Slaw

Servings: 3-4
Total time: 20 mins

Ingredients
- 1 carrot (peeled and shredded)
- ½ cup broccoli florets (chopped)
- 1 cup red cabbage (finely sliced)
- 1 green apple (cored & diced)
- 1 cup white cabbage (finely sliced)
- ½ cup of mayonnaise
- 3 tsp of raw sugar
- salt and pepper to taste

Preparation
- Combine carrots, red & green cabbage, broccoli, and apple together in a large mixing bowl and toss.
- Next, add mayonnaise and sugar to the vegetables, and combine well. Add salt and pepper to taste.

Fresh Exotic Fruit Salad

Servings: 4
Total time: 15 mins

Ingredients
- 2 tbsp raw sugar
- 2 tbsp fresh lime juice
- 2 tbsp water
- ½ pineapple (cubed)
- half a cup of blueberries
- 16 seedless red grapes (cut in half)
- 1 seedless orange (peeled & wedges cut in half)
- 3 kiwis (peeled and sliced)
- 12 strawberries (sliced)

Preparation
- Mix raw sugar, lime juice, and water in a medium mixing bowl and whisk until well combined.
- Cut and slice all fruit as described and put into the medium mixing bowl with the other ingredients. Toss and mix until well combined. Cover and leave to stand in the refrigerator for approx. 2 hours.
- **Optional:** add sliced almonds for garnish.

Apple Spinach Smoothie

Servings: 2
Total time: 5 mins

Ingredients
- 1 cup unsweetened almond milk, non-dairy beverage
- 1 frozen banana cut into chunks
- 1 apple cored
- 2 cups fresh spinach
- ¼ cup hemp hearts

Preparation
- Add all ingredients to a blender jar in the order given.
- Blend on high speed until smooth, and enjoy.

Better Then Fries - Roasted Parsnips

Servings: 4
Total time: 30 mins

Ingredients
- 4-6 medium parsnips (skin removed & thinly sliced)
- 2 tbsp olive oil
- 1 tsp dry rosemary (optional)
- ¼ tsp sea salt, more to taste
- ¾ tsp smoky sweet paprika
- **optional:** 2 -3 tbsp nutritional yeast (for a cheezie taste)

Preparation
- Heat up the oven to 390° F and line a large baking tray with a piece of parchment paper.
- Peel, cut the top of parsnips and cut them into thin julienne slices. The aim is to make all the pieces thin and similar in size so that they bake evenly.

- Coat the parsnips in olive oil, and evenly sprinkle with salt, smoky paprika (optional nutritional yeast) and rosemary if you are using it.
- Spread the parsnips on the prepared baking tray, making sure they do not overlap.
- Bake for about 20-25 minutes – until golden color, turning them once halfway through baking.

No-Meat Enchiladas

Servings: 4-6
Total time: 60 mins

Ingredients

Filling
- 1 can lentils or black beans (drained and rinsed)
- 3 cups spinach
- 2 tbsp olive oil
- 1 onion, finely diced
- 6 cloves garlic (finely diced)
- 1 tsp smoked paprika
- ¾ cup tomato sauce
- 2 tbsp soy sauce (low sodium)
- 1 tbsp maple syrup
- chili pepper flakes
- salt & pepper, to taste

White Sauce
- 1½ tbsp light olive oil
- 1 tbsp flour or (chickpea flour if gf)

- ¼ tsp garlic powder
- 1 yellow onion (finely chopped)
- 1 tbsp nutritional yeast
- 1 cup almond or oat milk
- salt & pepper, to taste
- ½ cup vegan cheese, grated (optional)
- 10 x 15 cm / 6" soft corn tortillas

Salsa (buy it salsa or use the recipe below to make it fresh)
- 15 ripe plum tomatoes
- ¼ cup of red onion (very finely diced)
- 2 tsp lime juice
- ½ tsp sugar
- a handful of cilantro, well chopped
- salt & pepper, to taste

Preparation
Filling
- Heat up olive oil in a large skillet pan, add diced onion and garlic and fry gently (on low heat) until the onion is translucent and the garlic soft and fragrant.
- Next, add the lentils to the mixture. Stir occasionally.
- Add tomato paste, chili pepper flakes (adjust the amount to your heat tolerance), soy sauce, maple syrup, and a generous amount of seasoning. Stir everything together and add ½ cup of water.
- Simmer the mixture gently for about 10 minutes, stirring from time to time, and all of the excess moisture has cooked out.
- Add the spinach last to the mixture
- Adjust the seasoning to taste.

White Sauce
- Slowly heat up olive oil in a medium saucepan. Once the oil starts to shimmer, whisk in flour. Keep whisking until the mixture is super smooth. Allow the mixture to bubble gently for a few minutes so that there is no raw flour taste. Be careful to make sure it doesn't brown.
- Slowly pour in plant milk beverage while whisking the whole time. Initially, the mixture may thicken quickly and look a bit

lumpy – don't worry; it will recover once all the milk has been whisked in.
- Once the mixture looks homogenous and smooth, whisk in nutritional yeast, garlic and onion powders and season to taste.

Homemade Salsa
- Chop tomatoes into small pieces – I cut them into eights and then cut the eights in half width-wise. You could deseed them first to make the salsa less watery, but I didn't bother.
- Place chopped tomatoes in a bowl with the onion and coriander. Season with lime juice, sugar, salt and pepper. Set aside.

Assembly
- Spread half of the white sauce at the bottom of the baking dish.
- Fill each tortilla the filling by placing the filling in the middle and rolling the tortilla around it. Arrange filled tortillas in two rows on the white sauce.
- Spoon the rest of the white sauce on top of the filled tortillas – top with shredded plant base cheese,
- Bake for about 20-25 minutes, 350° F, until tortillas look crispy and looks slightly brown in places or if you are using vegan cheese, look to see if it is melted.

Vegan Burrito Stuffed Pepper

Servings: 4
Total time: 25 mins

Ingredients
- 4 red bell peppers (seeded)
- 2 tbsp. olive oil
- 2 cloves garlic (minced)
- 4 spring onions (sliced)
- ½ tsp chili powder
- 1 cup of cooked quinoa – (1 part quinoa to 2 parts water)
- 1 can of kidney or black beans (drained & rinsed)
- 1 large tomato, diced
- 1 can of sweet corn (drained & rinsed)
- salt and pepper, to taste
- **optional extras:** guacamole, salsa etc.

Preparation
- Preheat the oven to 180C / 350F.
- Chop the bell peppers in half and remove the seeds. Add to a baking tray and brush with 1 tbsp. Olive oil. Cook for

approximately 20 minutes until slightly browned and softened but still firm enough to retain its shape.

- Cook the quinoa.
- Next, add 1 tbsp. Olive oil to a frying pan and cook the onion and garlic for 5 minutes on medium heat. Add the chili powder, beans, cooked quinoa, and corn and a tablespoon of water or vegetable stock.
- Remove from the heat and stir in the chopped tomatoes and salt & pepper.
- Remove the pepper halves from the oven, spoon the mixture into the pepper halves and return to the oven for another 5-8 minutes, just warm through.
- Serve hot with the vegan cashew cheese sauce drizzled on top. Enjoy!

Lentil Ginger Curry Recipe - Gluten-Free, Vegan

Servings: 4
Total time: 25 mins

Ingredients
- 1 tablespoon of olive oil
- 1 onion (diced)
- 1 tsp of garlic (minced)
- 1 tsp of ginger (peeled & grated)
- 1 tsp of cilantro
- 1 tsp of ground cumin
- 1½ tablespoons of turmeric
- ½ teaspoon of your choice of 'spicy' spice - chili or cayenne
- pinch of kosher salt
- 1 can diced tomatoes
- 1 can of coconut milk
- 1 can of lentils (drained & rinsed)
- ½ cup of filter water
- serve with cooked rice and enjoy with naan bread

Preparation

- In a saucepan, add in the olive oil, diced onion, garlic, coriander and cumin and sauté until fragrant and the onions are soft.
- Add in the can of tomatoes, turmeric, salt, ginger, and spices - chili/cayenne and stir to combine and cook for 2 mins or until bubbling.
- In a strainer, drain and rinse the lentils and add to the tomato mixture, mix and then add in 1 cup of water and stir.
- Bring to a boil and keep stirring to make sure the lentils don't stick to the base of the saucepan.
- Once the water has reduced and it is a thick mixture, add in the coconut milk and stir to combine.
- Bring to a boil and then reduce to a simmer until you have a deliciously thick, creamy curry.
- Serve on top of cooked rice.

Roasted
Butternut Squash & Chickpeas

Servings: 4
Total time: 35 mins

Ingredients
- ⅓ cup balsamic vinegar
- 1 tbsp dijon mustard
- 3 garlic cloves (chopped)
- 1 tsp fresh rosemary, chopped
- ¼ cup extra-virgin olive oil
- 2 cups butternut squash (peeled, seeded & chopped)
- ½ cup of baby spinach
- 1 can of chickpeas (drained & rinsed)
- ½ cup of raw pumpkin seeds

Preparation
- In a medium bowl, whisk the vinegar, mustard, garlic and rosemary to make the dressing. Whisk the dressing until well combined. Set aside.
- Heat a large skillet and add a splash of olive oil.

- Brush ½ cup of balsamic vinegar on the onion, pumpkin seeds, and butternut squash, and sauté vegetables until thoroughly cooked, turning occasionally. Turn off the heat and add the spinach to the mixture. Remove from the heat and allow veggies to cool slightly. Toss with enough dressing to coat.
- Season with sea salt and fresh ground pepper.

Hummus
Treasure

Servings: 2
Total time: 10 mins

Ingredients
- 1½ cups canned chickpeas (drained & rinsed)
- ¼ cup tahini
- ¼ cup lemon juice
- 2 cloves garlic (minced)
- ½ teaspoon ground cumin
- ½ teaspoon salt
- pinch cayenne (optional)
- ⅓ cup water, as needed

Preparation

- Put the chickpeas, tahini, lemon juice, garlic, cumin, salt, and optional cayenne in a food processor and process until smooth, occasionally stopping to scrape down the work bowl.
- Add water as needed to achieve the desired consistency.
- Store in a sealed container inside the refrigerator; the hummus will keep for 5 days.

Black Bean Hummus:

- Replace the chickpeas with an equal amount of black beans.

Beet Hummus:

- Omit the cumin. Add 1 boiled or roasted and chopped beet and 1 teaspoon (5 ml) dried dill weed.

White Bean Hummus:

- Replace the chickpeas with an equal amount of cannellini, Lima, or white beans. Add ¼ cup (60 ml) nutritional yeast flakes and ¼ cup (60 ml) jarred roasted red peppers.

Garden Lime or Lemon Hummus:

- Add ½ to 1 cup (125 to 250 ml) of fresh herbs, such as basil, chives, cilantro, dill, parsley, or a combination. Use additional herbs to garnish.
- Replace the lemon juice with freshly squeezed lime juice.

CONCLUSION

Making the switch to a NO MEAT mindset & lifestyle can motivate you to live a healthy lifestyle and to enjoy fresh fruits, lush green vegetables, healthful grains, and proteins rich plant-based foods that make up the bulk of a healthy, nutritious diet. It is totally easy to create a meatless grocery list on a budget with a little advance preparation.

You will enjoy eating this way as it is undoubtedly the best way to clean eating and to affordable way to shop.

Quick Advice To Stay On Track
With A NO MEAT & Healthy Eating

- Go carefully through the food labels, and watch out for high-sugar ingredients and sodium. By reading labels, you will be making better choices on feeding your body and mind.
- Choosing a NO MEAT is less expensive.
- The most economical option is to practice with the recipes included in this "So Yummy" cookbook.
- Stock up on affordable pantry essentials
- When you have the essentials on hand, creating so many options become easy.
- Not only will you reduce your grocery bill, but you will also enjoy the flavors and true tastes of food like fruits, vegetables, nuts, seeds and legumes.
- Making your own ingredients might sometimes be more economical than purchasing them.
- **It Can Be a Perfect Win**
- But an easy reminder – Fruits and vegetables are always available, and it's just not about saving money. That is an important factor, but the other major benefit of going meatless should be your well-being and reduce the risk of illness.
- Enjoy going meat free and the true taste of these recipes will be filling and satisfying.
- Hope you can keep with it, tell your friends because it is So Yummy!
- Check out my other books and my new podcast
  https://anchor.fm/crystal-jones53

Other Books You May Enjoy.

> Best seller

- **RAW RAW RAW:** The Next Level Eating: 101 No Cook Recipes
  https://a.co/d/e2mBGxp

- **Organic Homemade Skin Care:** A NEW LEVEL OF PERSONAL LUXURY - 101 Natural Formulas & Recipes for Radiant Glowing Skin: Beauty Inspired by Nature, Plant based, 100% Organic, Paraben Free, Eco Friendly https://a.co/d/aQ6EFnL

- **SUPERFOOD AVOCADO LOW CALORIE RECIPES:** That Will Guac Your World https://a.co/d/fc2S7iH

- **Put Your Best Foot Forward:** One Positive Guide to A Dynamic New You https://a.co/d/a6xOeB6

- **Ultimate Smoothie Recipe Book:** A Slimmer, Leaner & Energized You!: 50 Plant Based Recipes With Superfood Nutritional Tips https://a.co/d/dCqXZDk

- **POWER PACKED SMOOTHIES TEENAGERS WILL ENJOY:** 50 Tasty, Healthy, And Delicious Recipes https://a.co/d/9B8h2en

- **TINY, TASTY & NUTRITIOUS MICROGREENS:** 50 Wholesome Irresistible Superfood Recipes
  https://www.amazon.com/dp/B0BLZQJCWR

Big Thank You

May these smart eating choices improve your well being! Share your meals and love with family & friends.! And continue to fuel your body!

Crystal Jones

Made in the USA
Las Vegas, NV
30 October 2023

79867610R00079